DK eyewonder

Mammals

Penguin Random House

LONDON, NEW YORK,
MELBOURNE, MUNICH, and DELHI

Written and edited by Sarah Walker
and Anna Lofthouse
Designed by Jacqueline Gooden
Managing editor Susan Leonard
Managing art director Cathy Chesson
Senior editor Caroline Bingham
Jacket design Chris Drew
Picture researcher Brenda Clynch
Production Shivani Pandey
DTP designer Almudena Díaz
Consultant Nick Lindsay

REVISED EDITION
DK UK
Senior editor Caroline Stamps
Senior art editor Rachael Grady
US editor Margaret Parrish
Jacket editor Manisha Majithia
Jacket design Natasha Rees
Jacket design development manager
Sophia M. Tampakopoulos Turner
Producer (print production) Mary Slater
Producer (pre-production) Rachel Ng
Publisher Andrew Macintyre

DK INDIA
Senior editor Shatarupa Chaudhuri
Senior art editor Rajnish Kashyap
Editor Surbhi Nayyar Kapoor
Art editor Shipra Jain
Managing editor Alka Thakur Hazarika
Managing art editor Romi Chakraborty
DTP designer Dheeraj Singh
Picture researcher Sumedha Chopra

First American Edition, 2002
This American Edition, 2015
Published in the United States by DK Publishing
4th floor, 345 Hudson Street
New York, New York 10014
13 14 15 16 17 10 9 8 7 6 5 4 3 2 1
001—196635—02/2015

A catalog record for this book is available
from the Library of Congress.
ISBN 978-1-4654-1851-7

DK books are available at special discounts when purchased in bulk for sales
promotions, premiums, fund-raising, or educational use. For details, contact:
DK Publishing Special Markets, 4th floor, 345 Hudson Street, New York,
New York 10014 or SpecialSales@dk.com.

Color reproduction by Scanhouse, Malaysia
Printed and bound in China by Hung Hing

Discover more at
www.dk.com

Contents

Mammal world

You might wonder if tiny mice, huge whales, and humans have anything in common. They do—they are all mammals! All mammals have hair or fur, are warm-blooded because they have a constant body temperature, and feed their young on milk.

Odd eggs out

Most mammals are born, but the hedgehoglike echidnas (right) and the duck-billed platypus hatch from eggs.

Instant food

Almost all female mammals suckle their young on milk. The milk provides the best balance of fat and protein so that young mammals can grow quickly.

There are more than 5,000 mammal species

Hair (or fur) helps to keep heat in.

Extended family

Humans belong to a group of mammals called primates. Other primates include monkeys and apes, so they are our closest mammal relatives.

Open wide

A hippopotamus would be perfect at the dentist's, with its large mouth and wide jaw stretch. All mammals have distinct jaws, meaning that the lower jaw is hinged directly to the skull.

on Earth and the human species is just one of them.

Mammals are the only animals to have ear flaps.

Amazing mammals

Mammals come in all shapes and sizes, but those that look alike belong to the same group, or order. Each order contains different types, or species, of mammal.

In order of appearance

There are 21 different mammal orders. Most mammals are placental, which means they grow inside their mother. Some mammals are marsupial—these are born undeveloped and grow in a pouch. The smallest order is the monotremes, and they are the only mammal that lays eggs.

The dolphin's sleek body, strong tail, and flippers help it to speed through the water.

The camel's broad feet are the size of dinner plates and enable it to walk on sand.

Zebras roam in open grassland, where their keen sense of smell and sight warns them of predators.

Where do mammals live?

Mammals can be found almost everywhere, from the frozen wastes of the Arctic to the dry heat of a barren desert. Most live on land, but some live in water. All are well adapted to the surroundings, or habitat, in which they live.

The polar bear's thick fleecy coat protects it from the icy Arctic winds.

The jaguar's coat helps it to blend into the background in its lush rain-forest home.

MAMMAL MEDALISTS

In a mammal Olympics, the medals would go to the following: the *sloth* for being the *slowest* competitor—moving at less than 1 mph (2 kph); the *skunk* for making the *stinkiest* smell; and the *pygmy shrew* for weighing in as the *smallest*, at just $\frac{1}{16}$-$\frac{1}{8}$ oz (2-3 g).

Family life

Some mammals choose to stay in family groups, making it easier for them to find food and defend themselves. Mammal parents spend longer with their young than other animals.

Playtime tussles

Female lions live in permanent groups called prides and look after each other's cubs. The cubs play-fight, which is how they learn to hunt.

Meerkat watch

A gang of meerkats varies from 5-30 members. They are protective of their home, or territory, and have different roles, such as sentry duty or babysitting.

African elephants are the world's biggest land mammals.

Amazing mammals

● There are about 60,000 muscles in an elephant's trunk.

● A lion can devour 50 lb (23 kg) of meat in one meal. That's about 350 hotdogs.

● Ferocious fights can happen between rival meerkat gangs.

An elephant's tusks are just overgrown teeth.

Female families

Female elephants and their children stay close together in family herds. The biggest female, the matriarch, leads them wherever they go.

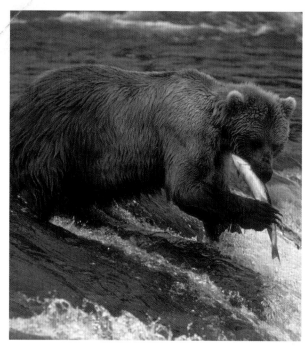

Different diets

What do you prefer? Vegetables, meat, fish, or a little of everything? Mammals eat all kinds of things. They eat because they need energy, just like a car needs fuel to go.

A mixed plate

This Alaskan brown bear, like other brown bears, eats a meat and plant, or omnivorous, diet. It waits to pounce on any salmon swimming upstream, but also chomps on plants, fungi, and large insects.

Keep on chewing

American bison are herbivores, which means they eat only plants. They graze on grass, and then rest. Then they chew on the grass even more.

Wild mammals build their daily routine around finding enough to eat.

Make mine meat

A pack of gray wolves mauls its hunting prize. As one of the world's best-known carnivores, or meat eaters, they have bodies designed for hunting other animals. They have powerful jaws and sharp teeth.

Don't stick out your tongue!

Giant anteaters wouldn't listen to this warning. They use their 2 ft (60 cm) spiked and sticky tongues to lick up termites and ants, once their clawed front feet have ripped open the nests.

The anteater pushes its long, tubelike snout into the hole.

Amazing mammals

● Wolves can eat up to 20 lb (9 kg) of meat in one meal.

● A giant anteater flicks out its tongue 150 times a minute.

● Brown bears eat a lot. The extra weight helps them survive the winter, when they sleep, or hibernate, for several months.

11

Moonlighters

Just as you are going to sleep some creatures are waking up, more than ready for the night. Nocturnal mammals often have special features—such as big eyes for seeing well in the dark.

Night babies

Bush babies have large eyes for night vision and batlike ears that help them to track insect prey in the dark.

The ringtailed cat is an excellent climber and hunts in trees for small birds.

Is it really a cat?

No! The ringtailed cat is part of the raccoon family. Like the red fox, it hunts alone at night.

TALE OF ALL TAILS!

Around the world, people like telling stories about me because they can't decide if I'm cunning or intelligent. In Ancient Greece, Aesop wrote about me in fables. In the US, I am Brer Fox, who tries to outwit Brer Rabbit, and in Japan, I am revered as a messenger of the Shinto rice goddess.

Night raiders

Red foxes usually hunt alone at night in woodland or open country, and increasingly in built-up areas. They will eat almost anything.

The biggest cat of all

Tigers like to hunt as the Sun sets and during
moonlight hours. Because their distinctive
thick black stripes help them to blend
into the shadowy forests, they are
able to creep up on prey.

Cats' pupils
expand to let
in more light
so that they
can see in
the dark.

On the defensive

When under attack, all mammals have ways of defending themselves. After all, none of them want to be eaten or hurt. Some will turn and run, while others will use unusual methods to put off a predator.

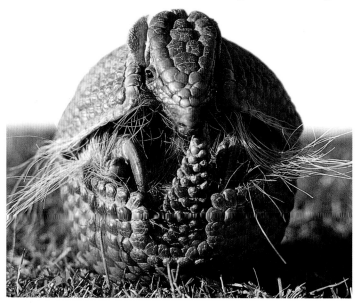

Is it or isn't it?
Virginia opossums often play dead when under threat, hoping that the potential predator does not want to eat a dead animal! They may lie still for up to six hours.

A living ball
If threatened, the Brazilian three-banded armadillo rolls itself up into a complete ball, protecting its soft parts. Tough skin and an awkward shape prove an effective defense against most predators.

No way through
These enormous musk oxen form a defensive line or circle, if threatened by a polar bear or wolf pack. Young or weak animals are protected in the middle of the group.

Fully grown adults may leave the line to charge an attacker.

Gentle giant?

The lowland gorilla is not an aggressive mammal, and what looks like a scary roar is actually a nervous yawn! Male gorillas will protect their social group. Defense tactics include roaring and beating their chests.

Underground, overground

Many mammals have underground homes or burrows where they have their babies and hide when there's danger. Most leave their burrows to find food or water, but some, like the mole, are true burrowers and mostly stay underground.

Busy burrow

Rabbits are sociable creatures and love to live in big colonies. Their burrows are large and complicated. They even have emergency exits!

Underground towns

Colonies, or towns, of black-tailed prairie dogs live in tunnels under grassland that may be an incredible 16 ft (5 m) deep. Prairie dogs line their nesting chambers with soft grass and dig out passing places along the tunnels.

Midnight feast!

These tiny wood mice are nibbling on acorns in the safety of their burrow. Their varied diet also includes berries, worms, fruits, and snails.

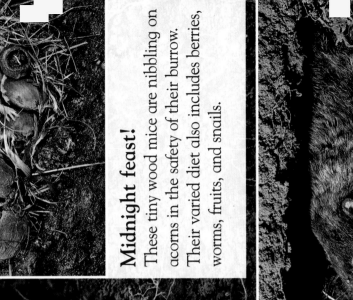

Tunnel vision

A pocket gopher spends most of its life underground. Its small eyes and ears, flat head, and long whiskers are all useful in a burrow.

Born to dig

You'll know there's a mole around if you see mole hills—a series of soft hills that the mole pushes up. Their huge front feet make them perfect little diggers.

The high life

Bats are the only flying mammals, and there are more than 1,000 species in the bat family. These furry fliers are divided into two groups: the small, mainly meat-eating microbats, and the large, mainly vegetarian megabats.

The biggest bat
The flying fox is the largest bat in the world, with a wingspan of more than 5 ft (1.5 m). It feeds on pollen and fruit.

Night fliers
A colony of Mexican fruit bats awakes at dusk and flies off to feed on fruit and nuts. All bats are nocturnal mammals.

Roosting together

Bats often gather together in huge numbers at a single site. This may be a cave, an old building, or a hollow tree. The site must provide the bats with shelter and protection from predators.

FINDING FOOD

Most insect-eating bats hunt using a process called echolocation. Each bat makes a series of clicks, and this sound is carried out into the air. This noise bounces off any potential prey, such as mosquitoes and moths, and sends information back to the bat. The bat can then find the prey and enjoy its meal!

Bloodsucker

This vampire bat is enjoying a tasty snack of donkey blood. Its sharp teeth easily pierce the skin, and its spit prevents the blood from clotting. Only three species of bat feed on blood.

Tent-making bats

These tiny fur balls are Honduran white bats. They only appear white under artificial light and are well camouflaged in the murky rain forest. They create shelters from large rain-forest leaves.

Primate party

Apes, monkeys, and humans are the most
widely known members of a mammal group
called primates. A primate party would
be a swinging one, since primates are
playful and highly intelligent creatures.

A devoted mother

An orangutan mother and
baby stay together for about
eight years. The baby clings
to its mother's fur as she
moves through the trees.
At night, the mother
makes nests from
leaves where she
and her baby sleep.

Gentle giants

Gorillas live in family groups. They are the heaviest of all primates but, despite appearances, are vegetarians. Their enthusiasm for eating forest plants and fruits can result in large potbellies.

A gripping tail

Many central and South American monkeys—such as this black howler monkey—use their grasping, or prehensile, tail as a fifth limb. With its distinctive howl, this monkey is one of the loudest primates.

Second in the class

Humans score highest for intelligence, but chimpanzees are second. This chimp is using a stone as a tool for cracking open palm nuts.

Amazing mammals

● The orangutan's name comes from the Malay words for "man of the wood."

● Do you like making faces? Many primates can make faces to show their feelings and to communicate with each other.

If you scratch my back...

... I'll scratch yours. These baboons are checking each other's fur for ticks and lice. It is part of a behavior called grooming, shared by most primates. This also helps the primates to develop good friendships.

Amazing marsupials

Kangaroos and koalas belong to a group of mammals called marsupials. A marsupial is only partly formed when it is born, and it continues to grow in a pocket, called a pouch, on the outside of its mother's stomach.

Mobile homes

A baby kangaroo, or joey, is born after just 12 days inside its mother. It crawls through its mother's fur and into a special place called a pouch. It stays in its mother's pouch, drinking her milk, for the next six months.

When the kangaroo hops, a long tail helps it to balance.

Thirsty work

A newborn kangaroo is blind, helpless, and very pink. It clings tightly to its mother's fur and will suckle continually.

Piggyback, please

A koala spends most of its life in eucalyptus trees. It sleeps for up to 18 hours a day and feeds only on eucalyptus leaves. A baby koala lives in its mother's pouch for about six months before crawling onto her back.

A fully grown kangaroo is as tall as an adult human, but at birth it is less than ¾ in (2 cm) long.

Powerful kangaroos

The largest living marsupials, red kangaroos live in Australia. They live in groups of about 2-10 animals, with one dominant male and several females. When bounding at full speed, kangaroos can reach speeds of about 30 mph (50 kph).

WINNER TAKES THE GIRL

Male kangaroos sometimes fight over females. This fighting can take the form of "boxing." The kangaroos stand up on their hind legs and attempt to push their opponent off balance by jabbing him or locking forearms. The winner of the boxing match is the stronger male, and he gets the girl!

Deep in the jungle

Imagine a place where it rains every day but where it is uncomfortably hot and sticky. Many mammals make a good home here among the towering trees of the rain forest.

Jungle jaguar
Hunting alone in the Amazon forests, a jaguar stalks prey on the ground, up in trees, and in water. This means its varied diet includes deer, monkeys, and turtles. Aside from man, this big cat has no rival predator.

All-day snoozer

You may not spot a sloth in the thick rain-forest foliage. It moves slowly and spends most of its time sleeping. Added to that, algae grow on its coat, causing its fur to look green. This young sloth will cling to its mother for six months.

Hooked up

A silky anteater's hooklike claws are ideal for gripping a branch. It uses its red, sticky, saliva-coated tongue to scoop up ants from their nests.

A trunklike nose gives the tapir a good sense of smell.

In the swim

Find a rain-forest river or swamp and you may spot a tapir. This timid creature likes to cool off in water and uses it to hide from predators.

Eye eye!

Pads on the ends of a tarsier's fingers and toes help it to grip a branch while its big eyes scan the forest floor for insects to eat. Can you believe that each eye is heavier than its brain!

Forest-dwellers

Unlike a rain forest, a temperate forest is ruled by the seasons—as are its mammals. In the warm spring, the young are born. In the summer, they feed and grow. Chilly fall days see thicker coats. To survive the cold winter, some sleep, or hibernate.

What's for dinner?

One of the largest wild pigs, the wild boar spends many happy hours rooting around on the forest floor. Here it is looking for anything to eat, from roots and nuts to small animals.

Snack stop

Each fall, red squirrels scurry around gathering nuts and pinecones. They'll store these provisions in the ground or in tree holes, raiding these "cupboards" in the winter when food is scarce.

Sleep tight

The dormouse doesn't even try to struggle through winter. It curls up, snuggles down into its leaf-and-grass nest, and sleeps, or hibernates, the winter away.

In the fall, the antlers fall off and regrow in the spring. They grow bigger each year.

Amazing mammals

● Dormice are named after the Latin word for sleep: *dormire*. They spend an amazing three-quarters of a year "asleep"!

● A moose has broad hooves that enable it to move through snow, muddy bogs, and lakes.

● The wild boar is the ancestor of the domestic pig.

Moosing around

The elk, or moose, is the largest member of the deer family. The male is huge. Its antlers alone can span up to 6½ ft (2 m). Forests with swampy areas provide the moose with all its food, but just imagine eating twigs or the roots of water plants!

Savanna plains

Africa's tropical grassland, or savanna, is home to spectacular groups of mammals. Life is hot and there is little rainfall, but grasses keep on growing for much of the year and grow back quickly after being nibbled on by the grazing herds.

Tongue stretch

Giraffes are the tallest animals in the world. Some males grow up to 18 ft (5.5 m) tall. Their long necks allow them to reach tasty leaves high up in the trees.

Predatory pride

Lions hunt many grassland mammals, even attacking young elephants and giraffes. They live in prides of 5-40 animals. Prides are made up mostly of adult females and their cubs, and include a few males.

All species of giraffe have different markings.

Amazing mammals

● Each zebra has a unique stripe pattern.

● Lionesses provide each other with a babysitting service for their cubs!

● Giraffes can gallop at speeds of 30 mph (50 kph).

Giraffe splits!

The short, wet season produces water holes that shrink as the year progresses. This drives groups, such as of giraffes, to travel great distances to find them. Their height means that they have to stretch their front legs very wide to drink.

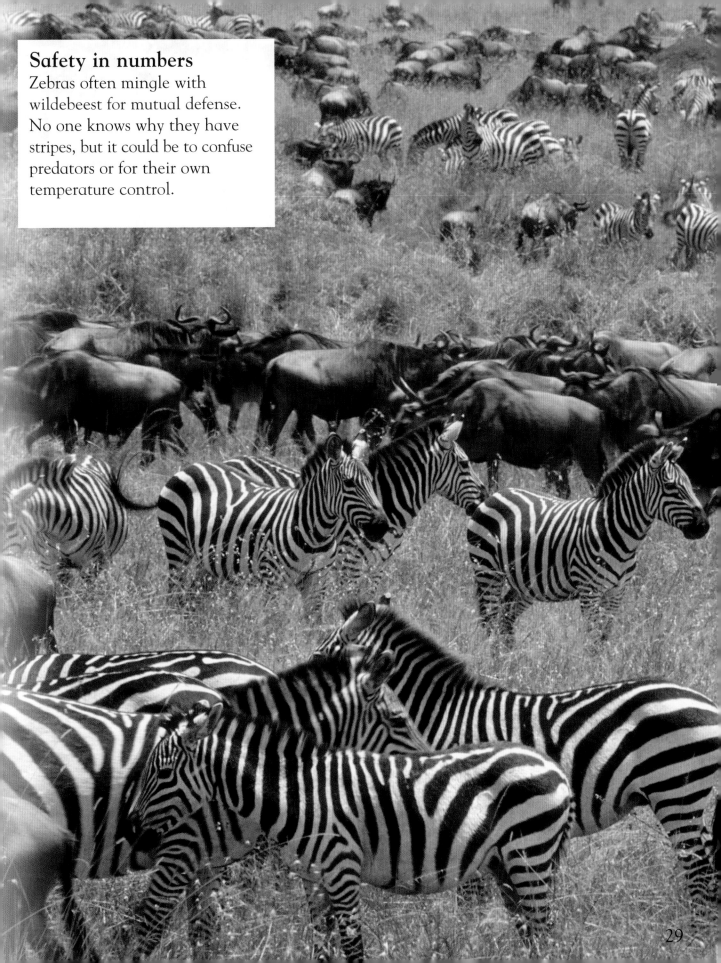

Safety in numbers
Zebras often mingle with wildebeest for mutual defense. No one knows why they have stripes, but it could be to confuse predators or for their own temperature control.

Desert homes

The Sun burns down. There is no water, and very little food. At last the Sun sets, but it is now bitterly cold. Welcome to the desert. Surprisingly, a number of mammals love it here!

Where's the water?

The spinifex hopping mouse doesn't need to drink. It gets all the moisture it needs by nibbling on plant food.

Ships of the desert

Camels are ideal desert mammals, whether they have one hump or two. They can survive for weeks and travel long distances without food or water, an ability that makes them useful for carrying things. That's why they are known as the ships of the desert.

Camels have padded feet for protection against the hot ground.

Cool grazers

During the heat of the day, Arabian oryx can be spotted huddled under trees. Their bright white coats reflect the light back, and therefore help to keep them cool. There were hardly any oryx left in the 1970s, but captive breeding has meant that hundreds have been returned to the wild.

Deserts cover about 20 percent of the Earth's land.

A double row of eyelashes keeps the sand out of a camel's eyes.

THIRSTY WORK

Contrary to popular belief, a camel's hump is *not* full of water. It is actually made of fat, which the camel can live from if there is no food or water. A camel can survive for 10 months without water and then drink a *lot* very quickly—almost equal to 340 cans of soda in 10 minutes!

On the slopes

A mountain slope is a tricky place to live. The weather gets colder as you head up and the air gets thinner, with less oxygen. And there's not a lot of food! But some mammals choose to make it their home.

A rocky home

Alpine marmots live high up in alpine meadows. If threatened, they make a loud, piercing whistle. To survive the winter, they retreat to their burrows to sleep, or hibernate, for several months.

A sky-high leap

The mountain goat is an expert rock climber, and baby goats (kids) can walk and climb shortly after they are born. Their oval-shaped hooves have a rubberlike sole that helps them grip onto the slippery slopes.

Many mountain mammals have thick fur to protect them from the icy weather.

Jump in!

These striking Japanese macaques live in the cold highlands and mountains of Japan. In the winter, temperatures drop below freezing. To stay warm, the clever monkeys have learned to take a bath in the natural hot springs.

33

Life in the freezer

The polar regions, at the top and bottom of the world, are tough places for mammals. They need to survive the freezing temperatures, especially in winter. They also need to be cunning to find what little food there is.

Boxing bunnies
Arctic hares have white winter coats to help hide them from predators. They have no trouble finding each other, though! The males box to claim a female.

Young polar bears spend up to two years with their mothers.

Polar giants
The enormous polar bear is one of the world's largest land-based carnivores. It has thick, white fur, which keeps it warm in the freezing cold and camouflages it in the white snow. Polar bears give birth to cubs in the winter in secure ice dens.

Made for snow

Caribou have hollow hairs on their bodies to keep them warm and thick furry hooves to stop them from sinking into the snow. Caribou are migrating animals, traveling enormous distances in huge herds in search of food.

Female polar bears nearly always give birth to twins.

Underwater world

Seals spend most of the winter in the icy water, digging air holes with their teeth in the ice above. They have thick fat (blubber) under their furry skins that keeps them warm while they hunt fish and squid in the freezing waters.

Freshwater mammals

Fast-flowing freshwater rivers and streams, large lakes, and boggy marshes are home to all kinds of mammals. Although well adapted to water, they all have to come to the surface to breathe.

An underwater playground

Otters are well suited to water, with webbed paws, streamlined bodies, and ears and noses that close when the otter dives. These playful mammals often chase each other and dive for rocks and shells.

A freshwater dolphin

This river dolphin lives in the Amazon River in South America. It swims through the slow-moving river channels, looking for fish and crabs. Sometimes, it swims upside down so it can see what's happening underneath.

Beavers are often thought of as pests because they dam rivers and streams.

The busy beaver

Beavers are nature's builders. They construct homes called lodges out of mud and branches, complete with underwater entrances. A series of dams built around the lodge controls the flow of water, so each lodge has its own private pool.

Lazing around...

The hippopotamus spends much of its life underwater and can stay submerged for about 15 minutes at a time. It likes to laze in the water, with only its eyes, ears, and nose poking out.

Beavers drag branches into place with their strong jaws.

Down by the sea

The shallow waters around the world's oceans provide a home for many mammals. Some divide their time between swimming in the sea, and breeding and caring for young on the shores. Others never leave the ocean.

Battle of the tusks

These large, male walruses are using their long, sharp tusks to fight over a female. Older males are often covered in scars from previous bloody battles.

The tusks of male walruses can grow to about 3¼ ft (1 m) in length.

Nearly all pinnipeds are covered in a layer of fat known as blubber.

A furry tale

Although seals appear sleek and shiny when they are under the water, they actually have two layers of soft fur. Adult fur is not as thick as baby fur, and some seal species are furrier than others. Fur keeps seals warm and is waterproof.

Dugongs were alive in the time of the dinosaurs.

A streamlined body makes all pinnipeds agile swimmers.

Underwater grazer

The dugong is also known as a "sea cow" because it grazes on the seabed for sea-grass roots. This large, vegetarian mammal spends all of its life in the sea, only coming to the surface to breathe.

Swimming sea lions

California sea lions are fast swimmers and can move at 25 mph (40 kph) in short bursts. They can stay underwater for up to an hour, using air that is stored in their lungs.

Leap in the deep

The ocean-dwelling cetaceans are some of the most specialized mammals in the world. The cetacean family includes all whales, dolphins, and porpoises. All have streamlined bodies, can dive deeply, and can hold their breath underwater for long periods of time.

Leaping high
Bottlenose dolphins are found in all of the world's oceans, except the polar regions. Living in groups, or schools, of 4-20 animals, these playful mammals often leap above the waves.

Breaching giants

This humpback whale is leaping high out of the water. This leaping is known as breaching. All whales breach, and we don't really know why they do this. It may be to warn off other whales, to communicate with their group, or just for fun. A whale this enormous will make a huge splash when it hits the water.

Water baby

Humpback whales tend to have their calves in the spring, in warm, tropical waters. The calf is born tail first, and its mother helps it to the surface so it can breathe. The calf will stay with its mother for about a year.

Friend or foe?

As in any big family, sometimes everyone gets along, and sometimes they don't! Humans can have close or useful relationships with other mammals. There are also times when mammals can cause problems.

A powerful snow sled
These dogs are Alaskan malamutes. Their strength, long legs, and thick coats make them ideal for pulling sleds over ice. They are very friendly.

Pesty nibblers

Some people keep mice as pets, but others squeal and are scared at the sight of them. House mice can wreak havoc because they spoil food if they get a chance to nibble, and they can eat through books and wires and spread disease.

Popular pets

Years ago, wild cats killed mice and rats that ate people's grain. Humans began to care for the friendly cats and soon they became pets.

A sheep haircut

Sheep were first used, or domesticated, by people many years ago for their wool, meat, and milk. Sheep are shorn once a year when their coats are at their thickest.

Wooly coats are valuable after they're spun into cloth or yarn for sweaters.

Under threat

Can you imagine having your home taken away or being hunted? Many mammals live with these threats all the time.

A watchful eye
Just as famous people have bodyguards, rhinoceroses have guards to protect them from poachers.

This black rhinoceros's horn can grow up to 4½ ft (1.4 m).

Shocking news
Rhinos are under threat because people kill them for their horns. The horns are used for making traditional Asian medicines and dagger handles.

A park for everyone

Large herds of bison wander and graze in safety in Yellowstone National Park in Wyoming. Nobody is allowed to shoot them. They share the park with many other mammals, including grizzly bears.

Pressures for pandas

A giant panda needs to munch on a variety of bamboo stems every day. Because of habitat changes, there aren't enough types of bamboo plants. Wildlife reserves in China have been established to help.

Orphaned chimps quickly learn to feed from a bottle.

Feeding time

Many people want to help sick, hurt, or unwanted mammals. These chimpanzees are cared for in an orphanage in Zambia.

Polar journey

A caribou herd is migrating in search of food. Help the herd reach its destination by answering these questions correctly.

START

the open

In the winter, polar bears give birth to cubs in...
See page 34

water

secure ice dens

four years

two years

Young polar bears stay with their mothers for up to...
See page 34

one year

thick coats

Alaskan malamutes have long legs and...
See page 42

rough coats

thin coats

find food

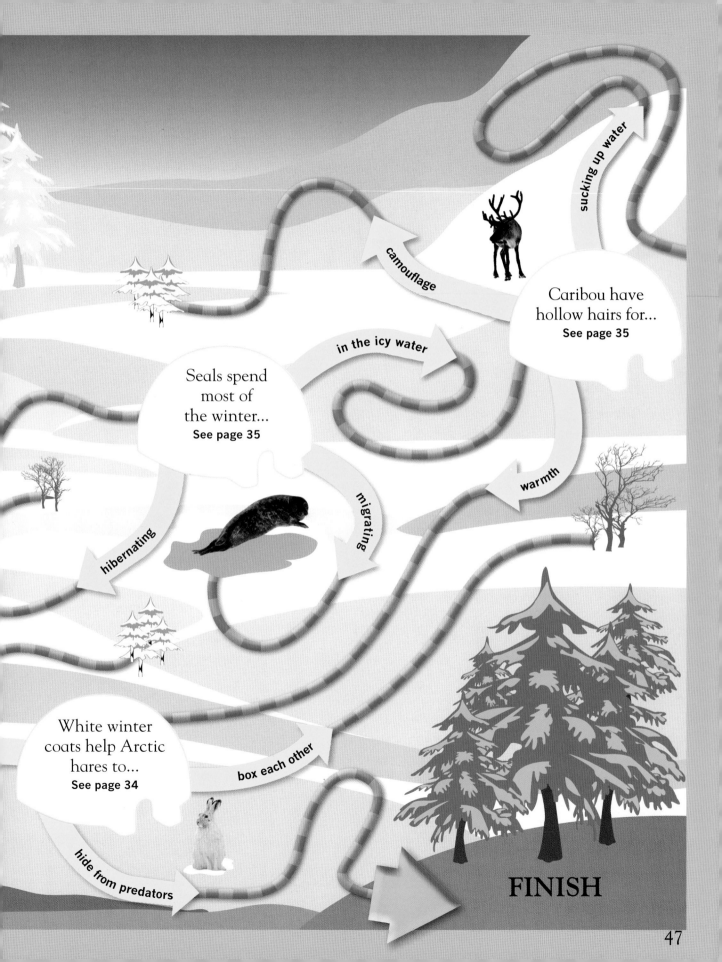

sucking up water

camouflage

in the icy water

Caribou have
hollow hairs for...
See page 35

Seals spend
most of
the winter...
See page 35

warmth

migrating

hibernating

White winter
coats help Arctic
hares to...
See page 34

box each other

hide from predators

FINISH

True or false?

Find out if you know these mammals well. Spot if these statements are true or false.

All species of **bat** feed on blood.
See page 19

Giant pandas feed on tree leaves.
See page 45

When an **opossum** "plays dead," its heartbeat slows down.
See page 15

Japanese macaques live in cold highlands and mountains.
See page 33

A black **rhinoceros's horn** can grow up to 3¼ ft (1 m).
See page 44

The **tusks** of a male walrus can grow to about 6½ ft (2 m).
See page 38

A dormouse **hibernates** during the winter.
See page 27

An **orangutan** mother and baby stay together for about a year.
See page 20

Camels have either one or two **humps**.
See page 30

Huge front feet make a mole a perfect digger.
See page 17

American bison are herbivores.
See page 10

Jungle safari

Have you ever been to a jungle? Play this game with your friends to experience what the jungle has to offer.

FINISH
Bravo! You finished the safari safely.

Find a shortcut through the trees.
Move forward 4

Drive along with swimming hippopotamuses.
Move forward 4

Rhinoceroses have blocked the road.
Move back 3

Follow an elephant herd.
Move forward 4

Get scared by a lion's roar.
Move back 2

Stop to take pictures of a chimpanzee.
Roll again

See a frightening gang of meerkats.
Move forward 3

Stopped to admire zebras.
Skip a turn

Wildebeest running toward you.
Skip a turn

How to play

This game is for up to four players.

You will need
A die
Counters—one for each player
Trace over the jeep outlines or cut and color your own from cardboard. Each player takes turns throwing the die and begins from the START box. Follow the squares with each roll of the die. If you land on an instruction, make sure you do as it says. Good luck!

Move down **Move up**

Get chased by a colony of bats.
Move forward 5

Rest a while.
Skip a turn

Run along with a wild boar.
Move forward 3

START

51

Who am I?

Take a look at these close-ups of mammals in the book and see if you can identify them. The clues should help you!

🐭 I am born after just 12 days inside my mother.

🐭 After that, I stay in my mother's pouch for six months.

See page 22

🐭 Using my sticky, 2-ft- (60-cm-) long tongue, I lick up termites and ants.

🐭 I have clawed front feet.

See page 11

🐭 I am an excellent climber.

🐭 I hunt alone in trees for small birds at night.

See page 12

🐭 I am a flying mammal, with a wing span of more than 5 ft (1.5 m).

🐭 I feed on pollen and fruit.

See page 18

🐭 Pads on the ends of my fingers and toes help me to grip branches.

🐭 I have big eyes, each heavier than my brain.

See page 25

🐿 My antlers can span up to 6½ ft (2 m).

🐿 In the fall, the antlers fall off. They regrow in the spring.

See page 27

🐿 Most of my life is spent in eucalyptus trees.

🐿 I sleep for up to 18 hours a day.

See page 23

🐿 If threatened, I roll myself up into a complete ball.

🐿 My tough skin protects me from predators.

See page 14

🐿 I am not an aggressive mammal.

🐿 My defense tactics include roaring and beating my chest.

See page 15

🐿 We are the world's tallest animals.

🐿 Our long necks allow us to reach leaves high up in the trees.

See page 28

🐿 We live in groups, or schools, of 4-20 animals.

🐿 We are playful mammals, often leaping above the waves.

See page 40

Glossary

Here are the meanings of some words that are useful to know when learning about mammals.

Camouflage a color or pattern that matches an animal's surroundings and helps disguise it.

Carnivore a meat-eater.

Colony a group of animals that lives together.

Echolocation a means of using echoes to steer an animal toward food and to build a picture of what is around them.

Habitat the place where a creature or plant naturally lives or grows.

Herbivore a plant-eater.

Hibernate describes the period some animals spend asleep in the winter.

Marsupial a mammal whose young are born undeveloped. It continues its development in a pouch.

Migration a long journey that some animals undergo each year to find better living conditions.

Nocturnal active at night.

Omnivore a plant- and meat-eater.

Predator an animal that hunts other animals for food.

Prey an animal hunted for food.

Prehensile tail a tail that can grasp (like a hand).

Stalk to approach prey quietly, so that it does not notice.

Suckle the means by which a baby mammal feeds from its mother.

Warm-blooded able to maintain a constant, warm body temperature, despite the surrounding temperature.

Animal alphabet

Each mammal in this book is listed here, along with the page number where it is featured and the area where it lives.

Index

Acknowledgments

Dorling Kindersley would like to thank:
Beehive Illustrations (Andy Cooke) for original illustrations;
Rose Horridge and Charlotte Oster for picture library service.

Picture credits:

The publisher would like to thank the following for their kind permission to reproduce their photographs:
a=above; c=center; b=below; l=left; r=right; t=top

Alamy.com: Steve Bloom Images 8-9; 21tl. **Ardea London Ltd:** Ian Beames 27tr; Liz Bomford 12cr; Thomas Dressler 28tl; Jean-Paul Ferrero 20; Ferrero - Labat 3; Chris Knights 43br; Charles McDougal 13; Stefan Meyers 43tl; S. Roberts 19t; Adrian Warren 19cr. **Bruce Coleman Ltd:** Bruce Coleman Inc 17tr, 24; Peter A. Hinchliffe 17tl; Werner Layer 27tl; Orion Press 6-7; Hans Reinhard 26; Pacific Stock 40; Staffan Widstrand 25tr; Gunter Ziesler 25cl. **Corbis:** Tom Brakefield 11; Bryn Cotton / Assignments Photographers 36bl; Michael and Patricia Fogden 25cb; Gallo Images 1, 4cr, 9tr, 28bl; Layne Kennedy 10cr; W. Wayne Lockwood, M. D. 32-33; Steve Kaufman 33br; W. Perry Conway 37br; Paul A. Souders 10tl; Kennan Ward 27br; Tom Brakefield 52cl; image100 49br; Kennan Ward 53tl. **Dorling Kindersley:** University

Museum of Zoology, Cambridge 49tr, 51cla. **Dreamstime.com:** Antonella865 50cr; Rinus Baak 48bl; Driescronje 51c; Iakov Filimonov 46clb; Jon Glover 50bl; Isselee 46cb; Mgkuijpers 49tl; Gentoo Multimedia 47c; Scattoselvaggio 47bl; Suzanne Weegar 48crb; Robin Winkelman 53bl; Simone Winkler 47tr. **Philip Dowell:** 6cb, 7cb. **The Image Bank / Getty Images:** Joseph Van Os 10bl; Art Wolfe 29. **ImageState:** 18l, 41b; Natural Selection Inc 44. **FLPA - Images of Nature:** Foto Natura Stock 39tl; David Hosking 45tl; Gerard Lacz 22-23, 42; Minden Pictures 22bc, 37tl, 39, 45tr; Mark Newman 37c, 38cl; W. Wisniewski 54. **FLPA:** Mitsuaki Iwago / Minden Pictures 52tr. **Fotolia:** Nadezhda Bolotina 46tr; frank11 51tc; Eric Isselee 53tc; Valeriy Kalyuzhnyy / StarJumper 50c, 50cb, 51tl, 51tr, 51cl; wojciech nowak 51bl. **Nature Picture Library Ltd:** Mark Payne-Gill 14cl, 31tr; Mark Payne-Gill 52bl, 53cra. **Natural Visions:** Andrew Henley 16tc. **N.H.P.A.:** Ant Photo Library 30tr, 38b; Pete Atkinson 6cra; Mark Bowler 21tr; Martin Harvey 7clb, 22bl, 44tr, 45bl; Daniel Heuclin 25br; Rich Kirchner 7cla; Alberto Nardi 6crb; Rod Planck 56l, r; Jonathan and Angela Scott 8tl; Karl Switak 16bl; David Woodfall 36bkgd. **Oxford Scientific Films:** Clive Bromhall 21cl; Mike & Elvan Habicht 14tr; Mike Hill 4tl; Peter Lillie 21br; Partridge Films Ltd 12tl. **The Photographers' Library:** L & D Jacobs 4-5b. **Photoshot:** NHPA 52br; **Powerstock Photolibrary:** 32tr; Brandon Cole 41tr. **Science Photo Library:** Gregory Dimijian 19bl; Phil Dotson 12cl; Adam Jones 5tr; Stephen J. Krasemann 18bkgd; Renee Lynn 28c; Phil Dotson 52cb, 53tr. **Still Pictures:** Klein/Hubert 23tl. **Stone / Getty Images:** Daniel J. Cox 34-35, 35br; Paul Harris 35tl; David Myers 14b; Art Wolfe 34tr. **Telegraph Colour Library / Getty Images:** John Downer 30-31; Tony Evans - Timelapse Library Ltd 16-17; Gary Randall 15. **Jerry Young:** 7ca.

All other images: © Dorling Kindersley.
For further information see: www.dkimages.com